DANIEL
in the Lions' Den

Adapted by Tess Fries
Illustrated by Cheryl Mendenhall

Art Direction by
Shannon Osborne Thompson

All art and editorial material is owned by Dalmatian Press.
ISBN: 1-57759-521-1

11451a/Daniel in the Lions' Den

01 02 03 LBM 10 9 8 7 6 5 4 3 2 1

Daniel was a
young boy
who lived long
ago in the city
of Jerusalem.

One day a great army came to Jerusalem and captured all of the people there. The soldiers took Daniel and many others far away to a strange land to work for their king.

Daniel was
called to work in
the royal palace.
He worked very
hard at all he
was given to do.

Daniel had been taught at home about God, and he prayed to God every morning, noon, and night. He knew God was helping him do his work well.

Many years passed and Daniel continued to work in the palace. He was always honest and wise in what he did. The king grew to love Daniel. He put Daniel in charge of his kingdom and Daniel never made any mistakes.

Other men working for the king were jealous of Daniel. They didn't want him to rule over them, so they tried to catch him doing something wrong. But Daniel only did what was right. Daniel knew that his wisdom came from God and he prayed faithfully to God three times every day.

The bad men knew they would have to trap Daniel into doing something wrong if they wanted to get rid of him. So they went to the king and said "Oh King, make it a law that for 30 days no one can ask anyone but you for help. Anyone who breaks the law will be thrown into the lions' den."

The king thought this was a wonderful idea. He didn't know the men were trying to trap Daniel.

Daniel heard about the new law, but he still went to his room to pray and to ask God to help him do what was right.

When the sneaky men saw Daniel praying, they ran to the king and said, "Daniel has been praying to his God instead of asking you for help. He must be thrown into the lions' den!"

How sad the king was! He didn't want to hurt Daniel. He tried for a long time to think of a way to save Daniel, but he couldn't change the law.

Finally, the king ordered Daniel to be thrown into the den with the hungry, roaring lions. He called to Daniel, "Your God, whom you serve, will save you!"

Then the king walked slowly back to the palace. He was so upset he couldn't eat or sleep. He kept thinking of Daniel trapped with all those fierce lions.

Early the next morning the king ran to the den and shouted, "Daniel, has your God saved you?" Daniel answered, "God sent an angel to close the lions' mouths. They have not hurt me."

The king was so happy! He commanded that Daniel be taken out of the den and the bad men be thrown in with the lions instead.

Then the king made a new law that everyone in his kingdom should pray to Daniel's God because He saved Daniel from the terrible lions!

Three times every day Daniel prayed to God, and God gave him wisdom and courage to do what was right.

God will give you all that you need to do right, too. All you have to do is ask Him!

"My God sent his angel,
and he shut the mouths of the lions."
Daniel 6:22
(NIV)